the skinscape voyeur

also by neil paech
the bitumen rhino
k is for keeper a is for – t.v.

no. 14 friendly st. poetry reader (co-editor)

the skinscape voyeur

neil paech

Wakefield Press

Wakefield Press
Box 2266
Kent Town
South Australia 5071

First published 1998

Cover photograph by Michael Constantinou
Typeset by Clinton Ellicott, MoBros, Adelaide
Printed and bound by Hyde Park Press, Adelaide

National Library of Australia
Cataloguing-in-Publication entry

Paech, Neil.
The skinscape voyeur.

ISBN 1 86254 406 9.

I. Title.

A821.3

Publication of this book was assisted by the
Commonwealth Government through the
Australia Council, its arts funding and advisory body.

Promotion of this book was assisted by the
South Australian government through
Arts South Australia.

contents

to penny, ann(e marie)
and the sparrow

acknowledgements

books and magazines
the fremantle arts review
the friendly st. poetry readers
the inner courtyard (anthology)
the southern review
tuesday night live (anthology)

readings
adelaide writers' week
beat route, the cargo club
boltz
the loungeroom poets, la mama (fringe, '94)
new writing performed, club foote
the railway family hotel, gawler
spoken writ, the crown and anchor hotel
tapas
writers' field day, mt barker
5MMM
5UV

penny

'if it was just a matter of skin
i'd say that breathing is not enough
beauty is just a word that carries shouting blood
through the veins of hubris like a crisis
of identity i know who i am is a question
of the exterior versus the interior of honey
my fingertips in yours as you kiss the exterior
of my cheek your lips take in my breath
i give you this bread
i make you the blood of my lips
that are the fingertips of words the tongue
is the skin of my thinking my face
is not enough i say inside the apple
i am green with honey you project
onto your fingers which lick my hands
you hold me in your hope i am more than
the projection of your desire on my face
i give you what is now unravelling
beneath the surface of my fingers
your lips entangle my skin
like hot meat on the run in the sun i am more
than just a mystery that unwinds in front of you
for the sake of your bemusement
you project onto the screen of my face
i am not you but me
i give you skin honey and words
for the quick quirk of your tongue
can you give me an atom of anything in return
too many take too few give
i refuse to be your waiting room passive with you
you give for a change'

a dream setting of a headland with a beach &
up above the beach an asphalt area & carpark
the plot synopsis i'm on the beach writing a
postcard to clare while she's still around
clare is avoiding penny for some reason i don't
understand she hasn't gone overseas as expected
& i've run into her after meeting penny in the
carpark penny has gone to the beach & i tell
clare but when she reaches the beach she doesn't
look for her so i'm angry & on my own & writing
a postcard to her asking her why etc i rip up
the postcard when clare approaches & walk away
i go to look for penny to tell her but can't
find her clare is trying to be apologetic but
penny has gone i've already looked for her in
various places & feel that she's now avoiding
me i also feel that clare has deceived me about
going she's with john on the beach

                                        her act of

her failure to turn up

my failure to attract her strongly enough
            so she would turn up

the walk past trees

            to touch trees with passing fingers
        is to avoid the feeling of cement

asphalt is just around the corner
            from the sky

                        the sky is part of the connection
of the tune of the tree with the tip of the skin
                as it avoids the concrete act
                    of not turning up

in the lack of development of the image
                        is the shallow film of the eye
            which won't touch further
                without denting

                                        deep

i'm due to meet her across the street at one and i force myself
out of bed at twelve-thirty. i'm still tired from the night before

i put in my contact lenses after cleaning them so i can see her
more clearly. i decide not to wash my hair. it needs to be
washed it's getting lank but it looks even worse when wet. it
plasters close to my head and i look like bone. at least it will
save time. i clean up the masturbation magazines next to my bed
on the floor. i clean up the masturbation tissues thrown under
my desk and flush them down the toilet. i wipe the toilet rim
of pubic hairs that have fallen off while pissing. i keep on
checking my watch and the time. i clean off the bits of shit
congealed to the yellow bowl with the toilet brush. it comes up
spotless and i drop down the seat. i have already shaved with a
new blade and brushed my teeth. i now shower. i clean off the
sweat and dead pieces of skin from the night before and it all
flushes away down the plughole. i dry myself. i dress in used
socks and my grey trousers with the darn in the leg. it is nearly
time. i look for a shirt and decide on the green one. it's bright
but it means ironing it and i have to shift some books and papers
off the ironing board to find some space. i begin to go over time.
i do my bed. the sheets underneath are crumpled and unwashed. i
clean the opened letters and crumbs off the kitchen table. i
sweep up the dead cockroaches from the floor near the fridge and
sweep them outside. they've been there for days

and it's five past when i walk out and turn the corner and see
her sitting at a table across the street. she stands up and walks
across to meet me. she stops to avoid the traffic and says as
she's approaching: 'you're late'

'i know'

i hold her camera and lenses. my fingers sweat
while we photograph the street. words wipe over us
like glass towels

our footsteps are filled with evolutionary tracks
which bark behind us. the human body
is a piece of slow furniture that digests space.
we skin the\difficulty of space.
we photograph it

the street is the lens we see through.
we see ourself

we chase glass out of our mouths that are dictionaries
of glass that break language into fragments
that define us

we sweat language

she takes photos of our steps into language. COCA COLA
as an umbrella

to take the bit between her legs in my hands
to lift her skirt and rubber her
to boil her mouth in the lava of my breath

(is)

the gasping of my feet
as they balance against the vertigo of her
(and) our headlong collapse into the collusion of bodies

sunset over the houses of parliament, london

    dear neil

     thought you might appreciate
the tackiness of this card. i did.
sorry i haven't written yet –
i think i'm finally coming back
into reality. i love london
although it gets depressing at times.
i've got some great stories.
will write soon.
i'm working a lot –
next to the tower of london
so beforehand i sit in front of it
and think of all the people tortured
and dead. it makes work easier.
take care

               love clare xxx

the shadow
in
the rain
drop

gear-shift
on
the floor

accelerate
(downward)

the fragility
of
the frozen
cloud

the red shadow
of the heart
poised
above the
glass
(lip)

almost
ready

(almost)

she lifts her dress. i have her lift her dress

that dress

that has the lithe fall of the schoolgirl
still

about it

and she lifts her dress and exposes her white

panties

she opens her legs up

a little

and i kneel down
and lick

her white
panties

the full on profusion of her cunt
the wetness of the white

as my tongue laps at the gap
which develops like a film
in a darkroom

light is white

and her picture clarifies my tongue

as i lap at her lips
open

with the breathing of breathlessness

the petite nature of her face
her wraparound skin.
she taps on the pimples
around her mouth
with her fingers
as she talks to me. does braille
with tension
in the muscles of her legs
as she stands and takes photos
of the poster on the wall
her back to me

HAVE A GOOD LOOK AT U.S. BASES
DEMAND A PUBLIC INQUIRY

vietnamese adolescents gather behind us
and talk in vietnamese.
they tap something out at irregular intervals
against the bricks
but we don't turn around.
the poster is ripped already
from someone tearing at it
in several places

SOVIET
BASES
OUT OF
BALTIC
STATES

is written in biro

and she takes long shots and close ups
of a black map of australia
with white names of white american bases
figures of blind justice
an american soldier
unbalanced scales
and a gun.
shoppers go out of their way
to avoid walking in front of the camera
as she shoots.
it is a soft war

the natural gravity of the situation is a dynamic of skin

the eye marvels to itself about the results of being other
than an imaginary being. the iris opens its hand to a gift
and the heart follows suit

the tongue is a volcanic flower that reeks of burning rubber.
the tongue. it does wheelies with hunger

it's too cold and wet to take photos outside
and she would've rather stayed home in bed

so we take photos inside the market of oranges and fish
and talk of icecream while eating it

she hopes the snow will have fallen in plenty of time
for when she goes skiing the following week

i tell her i've never seen it
and she rolls over the whites of her eyes in mock horror

so now i have seen snow

she touched my coat

just lightly
tentatively
a fingertip almost as if in passing
the ghost of an afterthought perhaps
but enough to make my bones
feel like lightning rods

the impulse that feels like a cathedral
the spirit is weak but the flesh is willing
something to that effect

whatever

she touched me and i remember.
days later

mount buller

friday 12 july

                 neil,

snow is ok
weather is nice
this is not a love poem
sorry about that
god it's nice to be
OUT OF ADELAIDE,

              pen

P.S.
    it's snowing!
    (SATURDAY)

the stingray lies on the boards
at the end of the jetty
a grey-black flat thing
like a nonsense of stigmata
without resonance
a red slash hacked down deep
into the heart of it
a dead stop naked
and open to the winds
of the young men huddled
against a raised blanket
which shelters them
from the sea hooked
into the corners
of their eyes

she dances on the dance floor of the jetty hotel
in a short purple cocktail dress that flounces out back of her

her legs pivot in their white stockings
and her purple panties shyly flash out

like raised eyebrows thinking champagne
a wistful moon through clouds

a phone-call)(contact(dis-

(the voice) hair) in the voice the lips around the word
(s) i take (sieve) them in (and (sleeve) sieve) them)
through my skin like (soup) (scalps of soup)

word water is words is skin is word water (is words)
is skin the sound of is (is a silhouette) that drives me on
through the (phone) machine (the machine (phone)
(is a machine is) is the voice on her lips
that (drinks and drives(s) my skin)

like (the) movie THE (on the make) (SHE) (ME) to be

(being) is drunk) (by drunks) (and turns light into mouth)
my mouth (her mouth)

the word world is a slow (warm) mouth (of) her voice)
accelerating under pressure (of) her voice

her voice is an engine that turns (syllables)
into perfect (mouth) pitch
(the idealistic mouth the idealistic ear) (perfect)

my skin (listens (to the) sweats below my hair (line)
i touch the machine and breathe (life) into it
like a myth of the first (machine) creation

(this conversation) is a machine myth (is on a roller-coaster ride
(to myth) i scalp skin to the end (byee!!

(click down (click (down) (click

ann

she works
behind a door

and i pass that door
several times
a day

deliberately

occasionally
i've even caught her outside
standing near the door when open
and it's given me my excuse
to smile

it's always disappointing
when i pass
and the door's closed

my life these days
is spent thinking mainly
about doors

and my eyes are windows
intoxicated with the idea of a position
next to a door

obviously
i am no longer human

her eyes are grey and full of the smoke and mist that follows
lakes around. i set up camp and take a drink

by breathing in and out.
my lungs burst into flame. i warm my hands.

my arms brown first. and then my face. under the heat of
her fired-up eyes whose skin i eat. she caresses my spine

as i scavenge her lips which taste
of the politics of action. she is a revolution of feeling

and my fingers burn when they torch like matches
against a box. and i warm my hands all over again

as her eyes examine me. i breathe and take another swallow.
i get my second wind. she reconsiders me. and ticks a box

which flares

a pool of shadow collects around her eye
and abstract thoughts rustle
as they edge towards it
to drink

coloured shadows slip quietly through the air
around me
as i walk around her eye
naked at last

her eye watches me from the shadows
and its coolness laps against my skin

i lick the moisture off my tongue

and her eyelid closes over us in an eclipse
of the everyday

we both stand stock-still
in the contact of our silence

i hear breathing. i listen to the night-call
of a dream. i hold out a hand and catch it
as it passes

she dreams my dream. i release it

we are in our element.
we are elemental

it was the first time
we had been naked
and together
and we'd done exactly the opposite
to adam and eve

ashamed
of all our clothes
we'd done a slow strip-tease
and stripped off all our cottons
and leathers and woollens
and our C20th god

we HAD left on our emotions
and fingertips
though

snake tight
skin light

and in our innocence
our bedroom became a hot-house garden
of darkness and growth

we were gardeners
and dug each other

i wait for her to ring. and she doesn't ring
i wait for her to come. and she doesn't come

i wait for her to come locked in my arms

i'm full of waiting
i'm weighted down with waiting

i'm like an empty cage
in which the air rattles against the bars
because it's too thick to squeeze through

i'm thick with her

these days other people have the same relationship to me
that i have with stone. distance

i'm cement. but do not pour
i'm set solid with waiting

and everyday i eat thinner and thinner
and grow heavier and heavier

i live in the ultimate dimension. that of waiting

though the waiting is almost enough.
at least i have something to wait for

i hope

she surrounds herself
with shadows

we are always in shadow when we kiss

and she hates car headlights
that penetrate her shadows

when she leaves me
she walks around a corner
of shadows

and she lives in a house
she refuses to allow me to see
because she fears
i won't appreciate
its subtleties
of shadow

in her room at night
i'm sure she commits arcane acts
with shadows

and when i hold her in my arms
i can sense the shadows of her ancestors
who take part in strange rituals
in the recesses
of her blood

her blood chants to me. i can hear it
through my fingers. and if she ever bleeds
i'm sure her blood
will be black

when she opens her mouth to talk
she releases shadows instead of words
and they slip sideways into the corners of my mind
where they hide away. and then
whisper to me at night
of shadowy things

she is always looking behind her
to check out her shadow.
daylight makes her nervous

and she wears dark glasses
so that the sun is always in shadow

she wears black
and is as thin as a shadow.
she stands in front of mirrors
and there is no reflection

her hair is a halo of shadow
and she carries a shadow between her legs

and when i have sex with her
i know i'll be having sex
with a shadow

but i don't care.
i have fallen in love with a shadow

and now we avoid daylight together

according to my wishful way of thinking
one night
as i'm lying in bed
she's going to pull up outside
in her car
and open its door
and step out

she's going to walk up to the outside door
of this place
and open it
and pass through

then there'll be another doorway
and yet another

until she's standing outside
my door

she'll pause a short while
and then open it
and walk through
into my room

i will then open my arms
like swing doors
and she'll enter that last patch of room
left to her

and then it'll be my turn
to go through her doorway
into her room

in the pub
she offered me peanuts
from the palm of her hand

my skin brushed her skin
which was moist and soft
as my fingers slowly
hesitated over which one
to choose

it was a delicately slow decision
and i savoured every peanut i ate

i've decided
if i ever write a sex manual
i will have a whole chapter
on peanuts

i had never known before that peanuts
could be so interesting
and i will never again take them
for granted

my only regret since
is that i didn't have the happy inspiration
to buy another packet
and offer them to her in return
from my palm

tomorrow
i think i will go out and buy
a packet of peanuts.
they could come in handy
at some future stage

sometimes
shaking hands
is one of the most subjective experiences i know of
involving two objects

it seems such a simple act

you stick a palm and four fingers and a thumb out
in front of you
and someone else does the same

you then have an approximate
mirror image

but remember
no two hands belonging to two different people
can ever be exactly the same.
and that's part of the surprise in the act
seeing how they'll fit

first the hands touch
and then the fingers and thumb curl over each other.
sometimes it is known as a form of kissing
with fingers

and when they unfold
they leave their touch behind

sometimes with the right person
you can sense the imprint for hours
afterwards

each touch is a collectible item
and is treated proportionally
to its emotional content

some touches can be very valuable
and are kept for an extended period of time
while others are immediately disposable

sometimes
shaking hands
is the only legitimate way of touching someone
while other people are watching

and sometimes
i would like to take home the hand i am shaking
to contemplate in the privacy of my own room

obviously
shaking hands
is sometimes much more
than just shaking hands

i pick up my mouth and dial it
i ask for her voice and she answers

her words stream into my ear

they are a black cord
and i slice it up with the precision of desire
into separate words
which i place under my microscope eye
which blows them up into the sight of sound

i swallow them separately
and they follow the thread of my thoughts
through my labyrinth of veins to the beast of my heart
which devours them, one by one
until the last
which slits its belly
and cuts out its tongue as it leaves
with the fading sound of her voice as its lover

i put down my mouth
and listen to the nature of the silence inside me
as it picks over the scraps of words for a sound

like the wind through bone buildings

patience is a strange animal
you keep on a short leash inside you
or it'll tear you apart

it's also a card game you can play against yourself

but i prefer it
when it's alive and well and no paper tiger

and over the years
i have come to understand this patience inside of me

such that, the other evening
when i watched them walk away up the st.
their arms locked around each other like a dam wall
and holding me back

and that patience inside of me opened up with its eye

i could throw it some breath and the bone of a dream
to keep it alive

i have time, i decided, and walked away. i can wait

there is a blue sky
beneath her skirt
like a blue smile

fresh with the colour
of being fresh with skin

and when her skirt moves
it is the movement of a smile
exploring territory

it is a smile of blue
with intentions all its own

and flows around her legs
with the art of pleasure on its lips

it is always smiling
with the smile of early summer

it is a blue sunday

and has no intention
of ever coming out

she says that these acts are just everyday acts

when she goes to the bank
or makes a phone call

when she buys a sketchbook
or drinks a cup of coffee

that they aren't anything special

but i think of the crush and crunch of galaxies on my back
with all their billions of suns and rocks
that move a million languages around

and i only knowing one

and the universe outside of her
and all those years like star clusters that will never know her

and that universe inside of her

and i want to yell out through all the screaming static
that here she is she's unique there's only one

and i want to break this static over heads like a supernova
as she flashes across my eye

for when she says that what she's doing is just an everyday thing
and nothing special
i believe otherwise

every one of them is an act of creation on the first day

and she is i am we are
are privileges to savour like a wafer on the tongue

her head is a mass of black flowers
that have broken through
her skin

their roots tangle
with her thoughts

and her smile is a breeze
that moves them around
in waves

she offers me one
and i break it off
and place it in the glass of wine
we share

she grows another
to replace it

and after she has gone
i drink the wine
and eat the flower

i steal the glass

she is a black lion.
she is restless with rage and cage
as she pours her feet into the ground for shift

she anchors herself
and tears up the earth each time she lifts a foot

she is a terrible sound
even when silent

her skin laps her muscles with violence
like a sea. she is so hot
it hisses

i kiss her and her lion-breath breathes with burn.
i scar with the hunger of meat.
i share her with blisters and she gnaws them

she is power and roar
and when she touches she explodes into claw

she is not safe

she is a white lion.
someone has painted her over while asleep
with the ideology of dream

we stand outside a cage.
she has freed us and we feed each other

our lips are raw meat
which simmer with our hotplate kisses

we have matched each other

our bones are now the muscles of love
and they hold us together

when i leave i have to put on my shoes

they are the terrible sound of skin ripped from skin
and when they walk they walk on stone

that is bone

to not be able
to touch

to have to stand
at a table
and not be able
to touch

to be able to talk
though
to be able to see
though
but not be able
to touch

the white horse
stands there
slowly eating away at
the darkness

its eyes are filled
with the experience
of iron bars
and wire
from fences

the darkness
frames it
and it tries to resist
by breaking the moon
on its back

the paddock has been grazed back
to hunger
and all it has to eat
is the darkness
of its own tongue

sometimes we grow used
to anything

a black tree
grows from her scalp
and has designs
on heaven

i climb among the branches
and pick the fruit

there is a penalty
every time you eat

i eat
because i have to

i knock on her dream

the black lion inside her pulls apart her skin
and stares me out
until her skin falls back into place
as if dropped by the wind

i phone her and she lets me in

i can sense the black breath inside her
as her body rises and falls
and i am the landscape outside her
as my back rains

the lion eyes me off
and its tail vibrates with thirst

her breast claws me

i am a black bucket
with a white handle

i stand in the middle of a vineyard
surrounded by vines
electric with hands

she fills me. she empties me.
she empties me. she fills me.
at will

i am at her disposal. i am
disposable

i am a white-handled bucket
standing on black empty
in the middle of a vineyard
of turning leaves

i am a black bone

i am full of hills and sky
and ground but not her

after five weeks
the vintage has been picked clean
and she has moved on
to another season

the sky is in grey and her skin in white
as she hurries below it

her eyes are leaves which smoulder
at touches of fingers which burn her down to a sky ash

she is in love with the body of autumn
and its temperature that fires her skin

she is coupling

we are the skin of the landscape inside each other.
we surprise us

we are the winds that wind the sky together

we are the trees of skin that are the veins of sky
that pump with breath the breath we breathe.
we breathe each other

we are each other's turn. we turn each other on

we are the rain and sun. the sun in shower.
the warm. the move. the laugh in weather

we are the eye of storm.
and the horses that run with rain all over our backs
onto legs and arms that graze each other down

our skin is the mouth that lips with legs

we are the hands that carry us. we are full

we are the land in landings

we are fused. we are the room of air
that weighs as heavy. we are easy

we build. we are built. we are builders and buildings

there is no end. we are no end. we are the point
of no return

we rain all over each other.
we lay in each other's arms and as we move we rain.
our skin is grey with weather

we have opened each other up and found the rain inside,
waiting. and as we move towards each other
it meets us half-way

our tongues are lightning
and as we lay in each other's arms
we listen to the rain on our skin

our breathing is wet with it as it falls all over us
and when we open our mouths to talk
it rains inside us

and runs on down our throats to our legs and feet
which twine around each other like the rain in wind.
it fills us

and our eyes are our gauges of depth for each other.
we read them. and when we have read them
we rain some more

she is a maker
of rain

and when she lies in my arms
i can hear the rain
beneath her skin

it is the sound
of muscle on bone

her breath is the wind
and her heart-beat the thunder

her face is a weather-map
of emotions
and her eyes are the skies

sometimes she is storm
sometimes just drift
and sun

but she is always full
of promise
never dry

and when i am with her
i am never in drought

every word is an incantation
to rain
and her lips are dancers

for she is a rain-maker

and because i am in love with rain
i never hold back.
i run in it

her eyes are the laugh
in her smile

they are magnets of colour
that absorb her surroundings

they leave nothing
but outlines

and flash
with a cubist's dream

they are orange and red
blue and brown
green and grey

they are lava with lines

she wears dark glasses
that peel the colours off of fruit
and vegetables

she buys black

black apples
black onions
black lemons
and a black cucumber

even the cheese is black

her guest is about to lie
on beaches of white sand

but tonight
she will feed him black food
and prepare him for his shape
in the sun

she has white thoughts

her words are a composition
of steel

and her sentences so heavy
they sink

they are a sculpture of rectangles
that lie on the floor
in a geometric series

they are equidistantly apart
immobile
and aggressive

and if you fall on them
you break

they are painted black
and i listen to their silence

to walk around them
is to be absorbed

to stand over them
is to catch only a hint
of reflection. everything is indirect

they fold upwards at one end
and look like mountain ridges
from which dialogue might flow

they are constructions of fingerprint
and nail

i walk

she calls

i turn

we talk
together
we walk
together
we arrive
together
we sit
together
we eat
together
we laugh
together
we drink
together
we toilet

apart

we leave
together
we walk
together
we talk
together
we shop
together
we part

she walks

i walk

we think
together

apart

that mannequin
in white
she says

that white face
she says

white face
white face
white face
she says

i'm in favour
she says

in favour
in favour
in flavour
she says

the moment
she says

the moment
the flavour
the moment
the favour
she says

the flavour
in favour
she says

and i
agree

lick

when i'm away from her for just one day
i climb down into that day like a black hole
and pull its gravity up over my head
and slowly sink into myself

i lose all my edges
and start to eat myself

i start at my bowels
and move up through my stomach to my head
which i suck out like an oyster in bone
until all that's left is my mouth.
until even that goes

and that's only the first day. the second
doesn't bear thinking about

we talk
and lean against the autumn light, relaxing

i leave my clothes

i dive into her eyes, and splash her eyelids with reflections

i swim backwards and forwards. i look out at light

i am warm. her eyes are artesian

with a splash she follows me in, my eyes,
and we swim around together, inside each other

we stroke each other's eyes

we play a game of hide-and-seek with laughter

we wear each other's skin. two skins around one idea, us

and we splash each other with language, and the thought
of touch

but don't

our words rub up against each other

and we eat each other's light. drink each other's breathing.
taste each other's salt

but there is no drowning, only saving

and we are not about to leave, unless induced

black

black

black

black

black   black   black

black   black   black   black

black   black   black

black   black   black   black   black

black   black   black   black   black

black   black   black   black

black   black   black   black   black

black   black   black   black black   black   black

black   black   black   black black black   black   black

black   black   black   black black black black black   black   bla

black   black   black   black black black black black black   black   black

black black   black black black black black black black black   black

black   black black black black black black black black black black black

black   black black black black black black black black black black black   black   bla

black black blackblack black black black black black black black black   black

black   black black black black black black black black black black black black   black

black   black black black black black black black black black black black black black

black black black black black black black black black black black black black black

black   black black black black black black black black black black black black   black   black

black black black black black black black black black black black black black black   black black

black black   black black black black black black black black black black black black black

                    black black black black black black black black black black black

                    black black black black black black black black black black black black

                    black black black black black black black black black

                    blackblack black black black black black black black

                    blackblack blackblackblack black

                    black blackblack black blackblackblack   black

the   black black black black black black black

black   black black black black black black black

black   black black black black black black black

black   black black black black black black

tree   black black black black black

wind   black black black

                    black

her

hair

it was her white jeans, which made me notice her first,
(she was so far ahead of me),
before she disappeared around a corner

and it was her white jeans, which really stood out
through the traffic when i did reach the st.,
before she disappeared into the store across from me

and it was her white jeans i looked for in the mall
after i'd lost her. but no go

though i did manage to catch up with her, eventually,
sitting in the window of her usual coffee shop

and 'mockingly' pointing out to me the red wine stains
from the night before at the pub,
when that drunk had jostled me

and then the switch of our talk to other things, as usual,
before our separating, as usual

and, as usual,
the concrete hitting up through the veins of my feet
and leaving me with that cemented-in feeling

of feeling sick inside
and feeling like bashing my head against the nearest tree

but instead, of course,
ending up at a pub drinking clarets,
and dreaming of her white jeans being close enough
to spill red wine all over them, once again

and the taste of white jeans in my mouth,
as i drank

her skin
    is so transparent
the sun shines through her

she warms me
    and i emerge
from my nuclear winter

she is so alive
    i imprint her onto my skin
and she absorbs me
    pore by pore

the space between us
    is a dictionary of collusions
that spell us out
    touch by touch

for once i am all correct
    10 out of 10

she is so alive
i live by osmosis

my breath rolls over her body
and lounges there
　　like mist

my fingers cruise through it
like curious tourists

　　　　looking to find for free
　　　　what they can't buy

they are skinscape voyeurs

but her hands are pieces of a catholic god
that puts them back in their place
　　　　with the tree of slap
　　　　and the weather of no

they are a headlight trip
brought to a dead stop

　　　　they are buried in hands

　　　　and my thoughts
are towed away for dismantling
　　　　into spare parts
　　　　for other nights

so that now
　　　　there is this relationship
between my fingers
　　　　my breath
　　and my thoughts
　　　　that is incomplete

her skin

winds wind down and fall and shatter

asphalt crawls and lies to shadows

pipelines move and catch at feet

whispers predominate. executives lunch

food coughs and suits die

glass cries and people consume it

hands run and windows listen

trees talk. we are all outsiders

tongues perch and clouds lick

paper is poison and bodies respond

ledges are birds and feathers heavy

performance is relative. the wardrobe wins

typewriters are phones and the word gets out

letters are drinkers and the word gets in

performance is passion and the sky shouts

the air is human. statistics flower

the traffic laughs and people colour

stone is active. zero is

she cuts her hair and a city collapses

i am a flat interminable horizon
when she isn't present

i am a flat road leading up to a horizon
i can't contact. i am flatter than flat

i lead on and on and on and on
into the recklessness of boredom

i am 4 flat tyres. i am 2 flat feet

there is no distinction in being alive
when she isn't present

and i feel like
every vehicle and pedestrian in the book has ironed me out
flatter and flatter
on their way through to somewhere somewhere else

i am an impression of tyremarks
that have left me for dead

i am in trouble with travel

i am a fly's wing

an argument
that is ephemeral and arid

and my words are scratchmarks along a line
that has no rain to offer

my colour has run out

and i have been left with a silhouette of boredom
after a nuclear blast

that blast of her

being without her is flat country.
and it grows nothing but horizons

she sits in a window and contemplates her coffee.
she is on display

she is an enigma
that has slipped back inside her smile

she has shut up shop and locked her lips away.
she sits inside counting out her words
and all i do is windowshop

i pass. i'm always passing

i'm that passing stranger you read about
who's a symbol of what i'm not. i'm not dark.
i'm not exciting

next time i intend to bring my lever
and prise her lips apart

i will break into her words and steal some smile.
i will carry it off into the shadows

i will analyse it under a microscope
to see how it works
then cut it and sell it to passing strangers
who will get high and o.d.
as i do

i will watch and laugh

she laughs
and i peel it

it is the scent of juice
and the wine in eye

the weather
in mouth
and fingers

it is smooth
and fast

the quick off the mark
the trophy

it is the wall
and fall

the earth and quake
it is on the make

it is a romantic

it is the sts. on the loose
my ears and drums
and plays me

it's a sell-out

there is a whale inside my eyes. they are pregnant with bone and the fountains inside me stand in for its heart. they wash it clean like bones in a bone-washer and my words are black plankton, sieved from the breathing that surrounds us. they collect inside it and eat it alive. her eyes give mouth to mouth. and it rises

she is a runner

her muscles are rivers. her veins are trees

her arms are pistons. her legs are springs

her breathing haunts her. her heartbeats collide

her lungs are lights. her hair is traffic

her hair is ice. her lips are breakers

her face is sauna. her back is sweat

her footsteps are warm. they inherit the earth

her running is river. she eats the bank

she winds herself up. she winds herself down

she is a clock. in the landscape

she is a runner

it's that time after the rain
when drops hang off your thoughts

we reflect our bodies

my hand is tight between her thighs
and her eyes are pierce with me

her lips are horny with the red
of plenty

i am cat food. she is daffodils

and there's no one in the room but us
and the fire and rain

we are the confusion of the lush of lust
and can't last

we fall out of our tree
and off our minds

she takes a bite from a pasty
in the shape of a moon

and a flake sticks to her lips

she offers me a bite

but i taste her lips instead

and when she leaves me
she leaves me with a mouthful
of shadows

plus one flake of pasty

which is light

i steal her lips from her face
while she isn't looking

i'm a collector of fine art

i place them in my pocket
and walk the sts. with them

i place a hand in and stroke them
for good luck

i pull them out and lick them
to keep them moist
and prevent them from cracking

i take a bite out.
overnight they grow back
to their previous proportion

they're of mythic quality

they have the shape of a cowrie shell
and when i hold them up to my ears
i can hear them whisper

they whisper of love and the seas of desire

so today, i've decided,
i'm going back for more

in broad daylight the sun is black

the black rose is a machine that never rusts

it has an engine made of glass and image
that runs on a mixture of blood and bone

its blood is for colour and its bone emotion

it always runs backwards in time. never forwards

it is sharpedged and caustic. it believes
in purity not parity

it carries concern on its sleeve. it is irrelevant
to desire

it runs it runs it runs it runs
on nothing but transience and word of mouth

it means nothing. it means something

it is always solidly sad. never air

the rose the rose the rose the rose
the machine of the heart that is almost enough

but not quite

he lives with her
full time

but
basically
he believes
that sex is the act
of an animal

he lives
on a higher plane

and i wish he would
take off

her silence injects me with the wind of a word
that boots me apart
like a puffball kicked in passing

i am the boot in question
that kicks me around while playing
with silence and answers

she is the silence inside the credo of silence

and i am a hand in a space called clock
that moves against me

i am the fingers of the hand that moves
entangled with hair

that pulls me apart as it pulls me with me

i listen
and hear a vacuum of wind

i look for panic and have found it

there must be a flipside. and i reach for the needle

he pulls up in her car and stands looking at the meter.
i arrive by foot and stand looking in the coffee shop

we cross the street in opposite directions

there is no language. only the process of silence
between the words of our feet

we are like siamese twins that pull in opposite directions

we consist of movements ripped from bodies. and there
is only the swinging thud of the breathing between us
to suggest we've connected

'bimbo. he was dark brown
and about 20 years old
just ripe for full retirement
and his last days spent eating
in the sun in his paddock
he was as puffed up as a well-kicked football
but ruthy and her friend found him
belonging to a woman who lived nearby
and they pestered him for 2 or 3 years
down in that paddock of his
feeding him grass
combing and brushing him
kissing him and talking to him for hours on end
and when they rode him
he was so wide
that you'd see them with their legs all splayed out
the one sitting behind having to hit him repeatedly
with something
just to make him plod along
he was so stubborn
he wouldn't move otherwise
just wanted to stand still and eat
that was his great ambition
and then he died
of too much grass
he couldn't digest some grass
and when he tried to cough it up
it stuck in his throat in a ball
and he couldn't breathe properly
it happens to animals quite often apparently
and he suffocated
blew up to an even greater balloon
than he already was
and for weeks ruthy and her friend
cried their hearts out
they wouldn't let them bury him for days
but would go down to the paddock
and stand by him and look at him

and ruthy would go on about him
being a gutz a pig of a horse that couldn't stop eating
he was always being such a gutz
and eating eating eating
and she knew it would happen to him some day
but things change she's changed
and now instead of horses and grass
on the posters in her room
there are rockstars with long hair
and guitars'

she waves
and the separation between us
becomes a seize of horizon

it is so much more lonely the hunger
than that separation between her fingers

that i would rather lay a swimmer between her fingers
and become entangled
    than die with air

            too much
                the air

we are parallel lines. she is an unknown quantity. i ring her
and he answers

i talk with her and our mouths are electric.
we are powerlines that touch in the rain.
we rub against each other. we crackle and burn

we take care with our words. he is in the background.
and weighs up our words and emotions in both his hands
as he strokes our throats

we ring off. we disconnect.
we return to parallel lines. that touch each other.
and our words turn to stones in our throats which we lick smooth

he shuffles paper through his head
and carries around the words of other writers
stuck to his tongue

they speak for him
so he doesn't have to think for himself
anymore

a rumour of lips fills the cup.
i taste the aroma of a kiss

on edge

she sits talking to others at a table behind me
and leans into my parallel.
i could reach across and touch her. but it's barbed wire

our minds are on guard as we rub body rhythms
against each other. we contemplate words
to carry meanings across their suggestions

when she leaves it's on a first name basis.
she turns the wheel and drives off.
she leaves me her basis and takes mine with her

nobody says anything behind me
but everybody clicks over several more notches

a breath breathes inside her. his breath. not mine.
i attach a lifeline to her words and breathe her in.
a wind roars through my skin

an architect of fantastic abstractions
i build connections between us. they are phantom emotions

she shows me her feet gone brown
while on holiday with him. my fingers are white
as i touch them. everything is subtle and blends with bend.
word around word. skin around skin

her eyes absorb the room. they are vacuum cleaners.
she cleans everything off me. down to my last dream.
i go with the room

there seems nothing left of me to pick clean.
my tongue is a cobweb of bone. i am an echo of stone

i pick up the room and empty it. in my mouth.
we walk out. she drops me off her breathing
one breath at a time

i savour the chill in the air of my bones.
my thoughts are marrow i break into
and chase with my tongue

my eyes sweat. dreams turn to cement
and when i jump i bounce

i ricochet along my veins
and listen to her voice pull me back out of gravity
into a garden of glass

i refract as i hang in the wind.
i am the bridge of my own neck

my feet are obscure desires. the ground
and my skin are rivers i swim in

words are clothes of rain

her so-called
friends.
they swarm
around her
like sharks
in a feeding frenzy.
they'd consume
the sweat
off her bones
if they
could

i cut off my cock in front of her
and air pours out.
i deflate in my own arms

i'm in neutral. in limbo.
i'm in drift through evenings of semi-expectation.
i am half-nowhere

i have been silent for weeks. i give her space
and walk over my own body to avoid hers

i fall off the edge of my tongue and float.
i'm unable to grasp my mouth and hold on. it's intangible

i'm in a performance of myself. i am endless

i have become an abstraction. a fiction amongst the reality
of chairs and tables books and shelves. i exhaust myself
with food and air. i have become a fiction in my own stranger

dissatisfaction has sunk me like cement to my feet.
i am a pylon without wires to connect me

i perform somersaults to turn myself around
and nothing changes. i throw myself back. i catch me.
i throw myself back. i catch me

i act out some maybes. they're a director's notes. i am not
the director

i am half-a-chance. i am no chance
and can only half-accept it

she opens her legs up and i develop a film inside her
with hard fingers. her bones move over my skin

she performs the miracle of the tongue inside my mouth
as a wind roars through me.
she carries me around inside her breasts
like burning paper

we are bullets that shoot us with our own emotions.
we have to struggle with the speed of our acceleration

it is a matter of hell meets heaven and the devil
is uppermost. we are athletes of god
and our bodies are scripture

we ride apocalypse. and apocalypse rides us.
survival is irrelevant. and to lose is a winner

we're performers and acrobats. we juggle each other.
we're all hands. we hurl each other towards each other

we tear silence into sounds. and eat it. the end
is just another stage in our performance as we try
for just one more time

one more time is always just one more time
to show each other around inside each other. as we do it.
just one more time

one more time

my brain is a telephone surrounded by questions
i am too tentative to ask. who when where and why
are molecules i sense out with cautious words
attempting connexion

shadows collide with shadows and doubt shifts ground
like rubber bouncing off rubber. i dissect shadows
and open up half-words. i shuffle around
looking for edges to hang onto edges

her voice is my ear and my mouth a hesitant surrender.
i try to solidify and only come up with air.
i am a bouncing ball that follows the gaps in a sentence
across some other language

i try to catch hold of the breathing inside her words.
i use my teeth. the molecules sink around me
and out of reach. i have caught nothing but hunger.
i have caught nothing but teeth

we sit together
at the window
drinking our coffees

and watch
the passersby

we pass some comments

on the beauty of a girl
a jogger
and a fellow worker

the sky is a mixture
of sun and thunder

some drops fall
in vertical lines

and slice us
in two

we lift
and separate

the liquid nature
of her body
as she lays there
on the couch
the curve of her body listening
to the night before
in the winter rain
on the roof
of her mindscape.
a heater
in a room
with a cat
as she lays there
warm
and relaxed
in the curves
of the night before
the day after
as the winter rain sweeps in
and knocks

she opens up

i turn the corner and she's standing there

she's talking to another woman about a sheet of paper
she holds in her hand

and wearing that fluorescent green jumper of hers
with her hearse black hair

and between them that face of hers
that carries the gasp of lightning in its look
as she looks me up and smiles

then down again

my heartbeat a hammer at my feet
like whispers from my tongue
as i walk on by

and my back a die
on me

everything flaws.
she dances without me and the sweat rolls off him

i buy her alcohol and everything falls down around me.
nothing stays up for long. in the end it all slips out

my tongue is oil seasoned with pepper. i sleep with acid
and it etches me. bite by bite

i call her over from the lights and she sits amongst me
at the table while an umbrella shades us

the heat is sexual arson and sets fire to the concrete
all around us

stroking balls and raining cunts click away like crickets on heat
and silence is a rattle of breathing we undress

our words are strings.
we puppet and entangle and pull and pick

we suck away at personalities in the roofs of our mouths
and eat outwards towards the weather

i touch up the hairs on her legs
and something in her bends over for a second. before springing up

impossible to do. anything but live her. the miss. other women
the engines and grease. i am no machine i am flux. i can't

ignore her as she runs and rans my attempts to be. two places
at once. be nowhere. other women aside. have to. put to.

have to. i can't compete anything than them but nonsense.
while i tear the edges away. from her. me edges

and scar with the rational ations that take me. where no.
but the end into ruttle of wood. against thunk.

not wood. knot i. a behaviour of sex
and her. part partner of a part-time smile that smiles a smile a minute

sometimes. not pretty. this ugly.
but i want her

it is not just a matter of a fishhead
but a relationship.
she drives her red mini up the st.
and around the corner
and the fish follows my eyes from behind.
just a fishhead without its turn.
its tail is a strung thing on a string of bone
but there is no substance in the construct.
she thinks about me from a distance
with relief that i'm at a distance
and the fishhead blinks in my brain.
fish are no feelings.
you can cut them and cut them and cut them
until they bleed
but they are no feelings.
her bloodred mini drives up the st.
and around the corner
and i am not a bleed.
i am no feelings.
am not bred to feel a bleed.
me no bleed.
my internal organs are external me
and the knive lies on the paper.
paper is a blunt instrument that keeps the table
clean

more space she says. then she'll contact me

there is space between us. plenty of it.
and it's full of cans of words that go unsaid

her words drip like skin from the trees in my eyes
as i walk through the space between us. i rust

every word is a can of silence between us
that blows us apart. me apart

a nice time. a nice time. it was a nice time
was had by all. the issues of a nice time

a meat time a hair time a fuck time.
a fuck time was had by all. the memory of a nice time
was had by all the next day after the night day

the night before. let's try and forget it. impossible

he wears a fawn suit everywhere he goes. even to the toilet.
he drives a fancy car with lots of dials.
he has a millionaire father

he lets her drive his car. it makes her wet.
he says so he'll know she can drive it if he's under the weather.
he knows she's fascinated by bright things

she says they click.
gates click. bones click. bullets click

she says he's complex. she hasn't worked him out yet.
she's been trying hard

it's obvious. he's into external things. money. a fancy car.
his suit. her face

he's into money. she's into money

he's into the status of class. she's into the status of class

he rejected his parents. she rejected her parents.
they've never been able to renegotiate their parents.
they're still in there fighting it out somewhere

she thinks they're almost on the verge of understanding each other

she thinks

she comes and picks me up after the market. it's spontaneous
and we sit and talk in the car about her floating on air.
she's just had an orgasm and her body's all sky.
she's an elevator and still going up

even if she did have to shut her eyes and think of someone else
while he was stroking her. with his joking on leaving her
about needing to bandage his hand. and about the tampon
the doctor found rotting inside her. the infection and the smell.
dead animal. it must have been there for nearly a month

and as we sit there in our empathy and sun ourselves
i lightly brush her face with my hand.
her skin is the emotion of moon without the stone
and her voice trickles through my fingers like velvet on ice.
her hair injects my skin with her rhythm of breathing
and our bodies are a collusion of slow blue

it is one of those warm weather interludes on a coffee cup day
where everything seems right for a change. and the taste.
of sweet and sweat and nectarine

i watch her hair as it turns the light black

every drunk in the place seems to want it. they adhere to the space
between us and she becomes a shifting variable.
a whole face. part of a face. a lip and its luggage

i watch them play a game of solitude with each other
when they think they're together

later she sits at a window drinking coffee and i talk to her
about his getting drunk with his wife in the cafe across the street

his boss was killed in a helicopter crash the day before
and they play problems with each other

who wins out becomes the garbo of pathos

who gets to cry in each other's beer and on each other's shoulder
who can use a sympathy card to their own best advantage

who gets to go home with whom
that's what it's really all about

and these days someone else's death is just a charred carrot
you dangle in someone else's face and hope and pray they'll bite

death is the fuckhook you use to grab them by the balls or cunt
and drag them in kicking

i watch them on the pavement outside waiting for the car.
the rain rains. and i wash myself down by drinking chocolate
that might as well be cement in a glass throat. i jag

the car passes. something passes

we approach the door at roughly the same time from opposite directions.
it could almost have been choreographed.
she's holding his hand and i quietly smile at her. i almost choke
and walk in first

they follow sometime after. i'm at the drinks table eating
and she stands next to me. my feet are like burning ice and my hands
are atoms on fire. i'm a walking melodrama of absurdisms.
i crash into words head on like a ship into icebergs.
'hi' 'you're stunning today' 'it's a pity you've come with that guy
but that's life'

i order a glass of wine and she orders two. we separate
and check out the exhibition together

we engage in conversations and silences next door to each other
and at times we check each other out for irresolutions and their resolutions.
we walk through ourselves with the attitude of intruders
in somebody else's territory

i overhear her talking about the smallness of the city.
how you run into people all the time. how she's buying a house next year

for my part i plan to take a break interstate if possible

we chafe at the rough edges of our disappointment with each other
and when she leaves she merely nods and i nod back

it is all very civilised. rather too civilised if you ask me

i steal her cunt from her
while she isn't looking

i'm a collector of fine art

i place it in my pocket
and walk the sts. with it

i place a hand in and stroke it
for good luck

i pull it out and lick it
to keep it moist
and prevent it from cracking

i take a bite out.
overnight it grows back
to its previous proportion

it's of mythic quality

it has the shape of a cowrie shell
and when i hold it up to my ears
i can hear it whisper

it whispers of love
and the seizure of desire

so what

Wakefield Press has been publishing
good Australian books for over fifty years.
For a catalogue of current and forthcoming
titles, or to add your name to our mailing list,
send your name and address to Wakefield Press,
Box 2266, Kent Town, South Australia 5071.

TELEPHONE (08) 8362 8800   FAX (08) 8362 7592

Wakefield Press thanks Wirra Wirra Vineyards
for its support.